Uncle John's
ABSOLUTELY ABSORBING
BATHROOM READER®
The Miniature Edition™

RUNNING PRESS
PHILADELPHIA · LONDON

A Running Press™ Miniature Edition™
Copyright © 1999 by the Bathroom Readers' Press
(a division of Portable Press).

Library of Congress Cataloging-in-Publication Number 2002100728

ISBN 978-0-7624-1385-0

This book may be ordered by mail from the publisher. Please include $1.00
for postage and handling. But try your bookstore first!

Running Press Book Publishers
2300 Chestnut Street
Philadelphia, PA 19103-4371

Visit us on the web!
www.runningpress.com

Introduction

In keeping with the traditions of Uncle John's, I present to you our shortest introduction ever for the first Miniature Edition™ of our line of books.

Please enjoy the material contained in this book. It comes from one of Uncle John's favorite editions.

Go with the flow.

Uncle Al
www.bathroomreader.com

Uncle John's
"Stall of Fame"

You'd be amazed at the number of newspaper articles BRI members send in about the creative ways people get involved with bathrooms, toilets, toilet paper, etc. So we're creating Uncle John's "Stall of Fame."

Honoree: Will Simmons, a freshman at Duke University

Notable Achievement: Turning toilet paper into a political issue

True Story: In his first year at Duke, Simmons discovered that the toilets in his dorm were outfitted with single-ply toilet paper. Outraged, he decided to run for a seat in the student government. His single campaign platform: a promise that students would get two-ply paper in dorm bathrooms.

Simmons won, of course—students know what's important. After the election, university housing officials pledged to cooperate.

Honoree: Donna Summer, pop singer
Notable Achievement: Writing a Top 10 song in the bathroom
True Story: At a posh hotel, Summer was washing her hands in the ladies' room. She mused to herself that the washroom attendant there had to

work awfully hard for her money. It suddenly hit Summer that she had a song title. So she rushed into a stall and wrote lyrics for it. "She Works Hard for the Money" was an international hit that went to #3 on the *Billboard* charts.

Honoree: Jacob Feinzilberg, a San Jose, California, inventor

Notable Achievement: Inventing the ultimate portable potty

True Story: In 1993 Feinzilberg

came up with the Inflate-a-Potty, a toilet so portable it can actually fit in a purse. It can be inflated in seconds and is used with an ordinary eight-gallon kitchen bag as a disposable liner. He came up with the idea for it at a picnic when his young daughter suddenly "heard nature's call and found no place to answer it."

Honorees: Philip Middleton and Richard Wooton of Chantilly, Virginia

Notable Achievement: Creating a "commode for dogs"

True Story: According to a 1993 news report, it's called the Walk-Me-Not. The dog walks up stairs at the side of the bathroom toilet, steps onto a platform over the toilet bowl, and squats down to use.

Honorees: Chiu Chiu-kuei and Lee Wong-tsong, a Taiwanese couple

Notable Achievement: Creating a public bathroom nice enough for a wedding . . . and then getting married in it

True Story: In the mid-1990s, Chiu Chiu-kuei designed, and her fiancé Lee Wong-tsong built, a bathroom for a public park in the city of Taichung. According to news reports: "The couple said the lavatory, complete with elaborate decoration, had cost about

$1 million to build." Chiu explained: "Since the bathroom is the creation of me and my husband it is very meaningful to us and therefore we decided to have our ceremony in here." Not explained: Why seven other couples joined them, making it the largest group wedding ever performed in a lavatory.

Honoree: Bryan J. Patrie, a Stanford graduate student
Notable Achievement: Inventing the

Watercolor Intelligent Nightlight, which informs bleary-eyed midnight bathroom-goers whether the toilet seat is up or down . . . without turning on a blinding light.

True Story: Patrie introduced the device in the early 1990s. He explained: "When you get within five feet of the dark commode, it will sense your motion. It looks to see if the room is dark. Then it looks upward by sending out an infrared beam. If it gets a reflection, it knows the seat is up. If it is, the red light comes on."

. . . And some vital "Stall-of-Fame" info: According to the *Philadelphia Inquirer* Toilet Paper Report, women's #1 bathroom complaint is men leaving the toilet seat up. Men's #1 complaint is having to wait to get into the bathroom.

The Earmuff. When he was 15 years old, Chester Greenwood went ice skating on a pond near his home in Farmington, Maine. He nearly froze his ears off. The next day he covered his ears with a thick woolen scarf . . . but it was too heavy and itchy. So the next day, he bent some wire into ear-shaped loops and asked his grandmother to sew fur around them. That worked perfectly. So many neighbors asked Chester for a pair of "muffs for ears" that he patented his design and founded the Greenwood Ear Protector Factory in 1877. He became extremely wealthy supplying earmuffs to U.S. soldiers during World War I.

The Outboard Motor. According to company lore, Ole Evinrude, a Norwegian immigrant, got the idea for an outboard motor while picnicking with his sweetheart, Bessie. They were on a small island in Lake Michigan, when Bessie decided she wanted some ice cream. Ole obligingly rowed to shore to get some, but by the time he made it back the ice cream had melted. So Ole built a motor that could be attached to his rowboat, and founded the Evinrude company in 1909.

The Flyswatter. Dr. Samuel J. Crumbine of the Kansas State Board of Health was watching a baseball game in Topeka in 1905. It was the bottom of the eighth inning, the score was tied, and Topeka had a man on third. Fans were screaming "Sacrifice fly! Sacrifice fly!" to the batter, or "Swat the ball! Swat the ball!" Crumbine, who'd spent much of the game mulling over how to reduce the spread of typhoid fever by flies during hot Kansas summers, suddenly got his inspiration: "Swat the fly!" Crumbine didn't actually invent the flyswatter; he just popularized the idea in a front-page article titled "Swat the Fly," in the next issue of *Fly*

Bulletin. A schoolteacher named Frank Rose read the article and made the first flyswatter out of a yardstick and some wire screen.

Random Facts

In the 1800s, drinking "tea" made from boiled old shoes was thought to cure disease.

Leaf-cutter ants can build anthills 16 feet deep and an acre square.

More babies are born in the month of September than in any other month.

Take a guess: How many muscles are there in your ear? Nine.

Fort Worth, Texas, was never a fort.

Two most dangerous jobs in the U.S.: commercial fishing and logging.

There are more telephones than people in Washington, D.C.

Sleeping around: Louis XIV owned 413 beds.

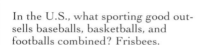

In the U.S., what sporting good out-sells baseballs, basketballs, and footballs combined? Frisbees.

If you tried to count off a billion seconds, it would take you 31.7 years.

Foreign Funds

Ever wonder why different kinds of money are called what they are? Why is a franc called a franc, for example? We did. So, we put together a list of various currencies and how they got their names.

Pound. (England) Named for its weight in *Sterlings* — the unit of currency in Medieval England. The first pound coin was issued in 1642.

Lira. (Italy) From the Latin word *libra*, or "pound."

Drachma. (Greece) Means "handful."

Rupee. (India) Comes from the Sanskrit *rupa*, which means "beauty" or "shape."

Peso. (Mexico) Means "weight." It was introduced by Spain in 1497, then adopted by Mexico and other

Latin American countries in the late 19th century.

Peseta. (Spain) Means "little peso," and was created in the 18th century as a "companion" coin to the Spanish peso (no longer in circulation).

Franc. (France) First issued in 1360, as a gold coin. Gets its name from its original Latin inscription, *Francorum Rex*, which means "King of the Franks," the title given to kings of

France in the 1300s.

Escudo. (Portugal) Means "shield," referring to the coat of arms on the original coin.

Yen. (Japan) Borrowed from the Chinese *yuan*, which means "round," and describes the coin. First issued in 1870.

Poker Odds

- Odds of getting one pair in a hand of poker: 1 in every 1.37 hands.

- Three of a kind: 1 in every 46 hands.

- A straight: 1 in every 508 hands.

- A full house: 1 in every 693 hands.

- A straight flush: 1 in every 72,192 hands.

- A royal flush: 1 in every 649,739 hands.

Slippery When Wet

Ice isn't slippery. What makes people and things slip on ice is water. A thin layer of ice melts when pressure is applied to it and it is this wet layer on top of the ice that is slippery.

The Outhouse
Winnipeg, Manitoba

Theme: Bathrooms
Details: The entire restaurant was decorated to look like a public rest room—"toilet bowls alternate with tables in the main dining room. And their logo, a toilet seat, was on all the menus." Shortly after the Grand Opening in the mid-1970s, health officials shut it down. The reason: "Not enough working bathrooms."

Alcatraz BC
Tokyo

Theme: Maximum-security prison
Details: "Diners are handcuffed, eat in cells, and must beg permission from the guards to be allowed to visit the rest room."

Dive!
Los Angeles and Las Vegas

Theme: Submarines
Details: "A submarine-shaped restaurant that specialized in gourmet submarine sandwiches." Partners included Hollywood moguls Steven Spielberg and Jeffrey Katzenberg. It had "millions of dollars in special effects," including "computer-controlled flashing light, steam blasts, deep-sea scenes on video screens, and

a surging water wall to re-create the experience of 'an actual submarine dive.'" Singer Thomas Dolby provided interactive sound effects that were just a little too real: "Apparently, the virtual aquatic experience was so convincing that it prompted an upsurge in customers visiting the toilet." The L.A. restaurant closed in 1999.

Truth or Urban Legend?

On an American one-dollar bill, there's supposedly an owl in the upper-left-hand corner of the "1" encased in the "shield," and a spider hidden in the front upper-right-hand corner.

Random Facts

First TV show to win an Emmy for Outstanding Drama: *Pulitzer Prize Playhouse*, in 1950.

Vitamin rule of thumb: The darker green a vegetable is, the more vitamin C it contains.

First announcer to say, "He shoots, he scores!" during a hockey game: Foster Hewitt, in 1933.

When mating, a hummingbird's wings beat 200 times per second.

Fast food: A bat can eat as many as 1,000 insects an hour.

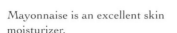

Mayonnaise is an excellent skin moisturizer.

Top 5 holiday pies in the U.S.: #1 pumpkin, #2 apple, #3 cherry, #4 lemon meringue, #5 pecan.

What do grape juice and the blesbok antelope have in common? Same color.

Theodore Roosevelt's boyhood friends called him Teedie, not Teddy.

Write this one down: The typewriter was invented before the fountain pen.

Strange Lawsuits

These days, it seems that people will sue each other over practically anything. Here are a few real-life examples of unusual legal battles.

The Plaintiff: A Chinese restaurant in Stansted, England

The Defendant: Kevin Clifford, a customer

The Lawsuit: In 1996 Clifford walked into the restaurant and ordered a large meal. While he was waiting for it, he explained later, the smells from the kitchen made him so hungry that he lost control. He began ripping the leaves off potted plants, eating them. "By the time his order was ready," according to one report, "he had eaten the leaves off every plant in the place." The restaurant owner sued him for the cost of the plants.

The Verdict: Guilty. Clifford's unusual salad cost him $700.

The Plaintiff: Nellie Mitchell, a 98-year-old Arkansas woman

The Defendant: Globe International, publishers of the supermarket tabloid the *Sun*

The Lawsuit: In 1990 the *Sun* ran a

"report" about a 101-year-old news-paper carrier in Australia "who'd quit her route because she'd become pregnant by a millionaire customer." They picked a photo of Mitchell to illustrate it. Why? They assumed she was dead. She wasn't, and sued for invasion of privacy.

The Verdict: The jury awarded her $1.5 million (later reduced to $850,000). A judge compared her experience to being "dragged slowly through a pile of untreated sewage."

The Plaintiffs: Two college students
The Defendant: Pace University, Long Island, New York
The Lawsuit: The students took an introductory computer programming course at Pace. One day the teacher required them, as homework, to calculate the cost of an aluminum atom. The answer, $6.22054463335 \times 10^{-26}$, is less than a *trillionth* of a penny. Outraged that such a high level of work was required in an introductory course, the pair sued.

The Verdict: Believe it or not, the judge found the instructor guilty of "educational malpractice."

American Traditions

There are some things Americans do . . . because well it's just what we do. How many of you know how these traditions started?

receive medals; it was unheard of to honor a common soldier for bravery. George Washington changed this practice. On August 7, 1782, he ordered the creation of the Badge of Military Merit, in the "figure of a heart in purple cloth or silk." (Purple was traditionally the color reserved for royalty.) The medal was awarded for "any singularly meritorious action," not necessarily for being wounded in action.

The medal fell into disuse for more than 150 years, but in 1932, to commemorate the 200th anniversary of Washington's birth, Gen. Douglas MacArthur revived it and gave it its current meaning.

Smell Facts

• Women have a keener sense of smell than men.

• By simply smelling a piece of clothing, most people can tell if it was worn by a woman or a man.

• Each of us has an odor that is, like our fingerprints, unique. One result, researchers say: Much of the thrill of kissing comes from smelling the unique odors of another's face.

• Smells stimulate learning. Students given olfactory stimulation along with a word list retain much more information and remember it longer.

- Many smells are heavier than air and can be smelled only at ground level.

- We smell best if we take several short sniffs, rather than one long one.

The Who?

Ever wonder how rock bands get their names? So did we. After digging around, we found these "origin" stories.

The Gin Blossoms. A gin blossom is slang for the capillaries in your nose and face that burst because of excessive drinking.

Procul Harum. Named after a friend's cat. It's Latin for "beyond all things."

The Boomtown Rats. Named after a gang in Woody Guthrie's autobiography, *Bound for Glory*.

Generation X. Named after a book that singer Billy Idol found in his mother's bookcase. It was a mid-1960 sociological essay by Charles Hamblett and Jane Deverson that featured interviews with U.K. teenagers in competing gangs called the Mods and Rockers.

10,000 Maniacs. Came from the cult horror film *2,000 Maniacs*. One of the band members misunderstood the film's name.

Foo Fighters. World War II fighter pilot slang for UFOs.

Rage Against the Machine. Name refers to a (hoped-for) reaction of ordinary people against corporations, governments, and other invasive institutions that control our society.

Hot Tuna. Originally Hot S**t. The band's record label made them change the second word to Tuna.

Dire Straits. Suggested by a friend who was concerned about the state of the band's finances.

Mothers of Invention. Frank Zappa's group was originally just The Mothers. But their record company was concerned it would be interpreted as an Oedipal reference and insisted that they change it. The band chose the name from the old saying "necessity is the mother of invention."

Pearl Jam. Singer Eddie Vedder suggested the name in honor of his aunt Pearl's homemade jam, supposedly a natural aphrodisiac containing peyote.

Beastie Boys. "Beastie" supposedly stands for Boys Entering Anarchistic States Towards Inner Excellence.

Squirrel Nut Zippers. From a brand of old-time peanut-flavored candy containing caramel and nuts.

Blind Melon. According to bassist Brad Smith, the name was slang for unemployed hippies in his Mississippi town. Also sounds suspiciously like an anagram of blues singer Blind Lemon.

Blue Öyster Cult. An anagram of "Cully Stout Beer." It was chosen by a band member one night as he was mindlessly doodling while at a bar with the band's manager.

Devo. An abbreviation for *de-evolution*, something that the members of the group believe is happening to the human race.

REM. An acronym for rapid eye movement. REM sleep is the state of sleep in which dreams occur.

Matchbox 20. Took its name from the combination of a softball jersey bearing the number 20 and a patch that read "matchbox." The name is meaningless. "The two parts aren't even related," singer Rob Thomas has said.

311. The police code for indecent exposure in California.

ZZ Top. Said to have been inspired by a poster of Texas bluesman Z. Z. Hill, and rolling-paper brands "Zig Zag" and "Top."

Counting Crows. A reference to an old British poem that said life is as meaningless as counting crows.

L7. Fifties slang for someone who is "square," or uncool.

The Who. According to legend, the group, first called The High Numbers, was looking for a new name. Every time someone came up with an idea, they jokingly asked, "The *who*?" Finally, a friend said,

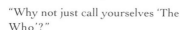

"Why not just call yourselves 'The Who'?"

Random Facts

The world's highest public telephone booth is on the Siachen Glacier, in India.

Ketchup was once sold as a medicine.

Toto the dog was paid $125 a week for his work in *The Wizard of Oz*.

Mona Lisa has no eyebrows. Shaved eyebrows were the fad when she was painted.

Founding Fathers

You already know the names. Here's who they belonged to.

William Colgate. In the early 1800s, making soap at home was a matter of pride with American housewives: 75% of U.S. soap was made at home (although it smelled terrible). In 1806 Colgate opened a soap business and succeeded by offering home delivery, and by adding perfume to his soap.

Gerhard Mennen. While recovering from malaria in the 1870s, he learned so much about the pharmaceutical trade that he opened his own

drugstore. He made his own reme-
dies, including Mennen's Borated
Talcum Infant Powder—American's
first talcum powder.

Dr. William Erastus Upjohn. Until
he invented a process for manufactur-
ing soft pills, prescription pills were
hard as a rock—you couldn't smash
them with a hammer, and they often
passed through a person's system
without being absorbed by the body.
Upjohn's invention changed all that.

John Michael Kohler. A Wisconsin foundry owner in the 1880s. One of his big sellers was an enameled iron water trough for farm animals. In 1883, convinced that demand for household plumbing fixtures was growing, he made four cast-iron feet, welded them to the animal trough, and began selling it as a bathtub.

William Boeing. When he wasn't working for his father, a timber and iron baron, Boeing and a friend

named Conrad Westervelt built sea-
planes as a hobby. In 1916 the pair
founded Pacific Aero Products. When
the U.S. entered World War I in
1917, the Navy bought 50 of his
planes. He never worked for his
father again.

William Rand and Andrew McNally. Rand and McNally printed railroad tickets and timetables. In 1872 they added maps to their line. Other companies used wood or metal engravings to make their maps; Rand McNally used wax engravings, allowing them to update and correct maps at a fraction of the cost. By the early 1900s Rand McNally was one of the largest mapmakers in the country.

Looney Laws

Believe it or not, these laws are real.

In Macomb, Illinois, it's illegal for a car to impersonate a wolf.

In Rumford, Maine, it's against the law to bite your landlord.

An ordinance in San Francisco bans picking up used confetti to throw again.

It's against the law in Atlanta, Georgia, to tie a giraffe to a telephone pole or street lamp.

It's against the law in Chicago to eat in a place that is on fire.

In International Falls, Minnesota, it's against the law for a cat to chase a dog up a telephone pole.

It's illegal to catch fish while on horseback in Washington, D.C.

It's illegal to take a lion to the theater in Maryland.

It's against the law to drive more than 2,000 sheep down Hollywood Boulevard.

Brawley, California, passed a resolution banning snow within the city limits.

In Tennessee, it's illegal to drive a car while you're asleep.

Anyone found underneath a sidewalk
in Florida is guilty of disorderly conduct.

It's illegal in New Jersey to slurp
your soup.

A Texas law states that when two
trains meet at a railroad crossing,
each must come to a full stop,
and neither shall proceed until
the other has gone.

It's illegal in Hartford, Connecticut,

to kiss your wife on a Sunday.

It's against the law in Kentucky to remarry the same man four times.

In Marshalltown, Iowa, it's illegal for a horse to eat a fire hydrant.

In Tennessee, it's against the law to shoot game other than whales from a moving car.

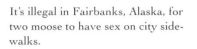

It's illegal in Fairbanks, Alaska, for two moose to have sex on city sidewalks.

Uncle John's Page of Lists

For years, the BRI has had a file full of lists. We've never been sure what to do with them . . . until now.

Titles of 4 Hollywood Films Re-Dubbed in Hong Kong

1. **Fargo:** "Mysterious Murder in Snowy Cream"
2. **The English Patient:** "Don't Ask Me Who I Am"
3. **Boogie Nights:** "His Powerful Device Makes Him Famous"
4. **Nixon:** "The Big Liar"

4 Names for Things You Didn't Know Had Names

1. **Aglet:** "The covering on the end of a shoelace"
2. **Phosphenes:** "The lights you see when you close your eyes hard"
3. **Kick or Punt:** "The indentation at the bottom of wine bottles"
4. **Harp:** "The metal hoop that supports a lampshade"

of tarot cards in fortune-telling is in Venice, Italy, in 1527, but the fad didn't take off until 1781, when a French scholar proposed that cards in the deck contained the knowledge of the Egyptian hieroglyphic *Book of Thoth*, which he claimed had been saved from the ruins of sacked and burned Egyptian temples centuries earlier.

Random Facts

If the average male never shaved, his beard would be 13 feet long on the day he died.

Experts tell us that the human body has about 60,000 miles of blood vessels.

Jackrabbits got their names because their ears look like a donkey's (jackass).

If you lined up all of the Slinkys ever made in a row, they could wrap around the earth 126 times.

Every thousand years, spring gets two-thirds of a day shorter.

If you weigh 120 pounds on earth, you'll weigh about 20 pounds on the moon.

Bet on it: Horse jockeys are the only

U.S. athletes legally allowed to bet on themselves.

Your odds of living to 116: 1 in 2 billion.

New data: The average American man laughs 69 times a day; the average woman, 55.

First nationwide best-selling book in the U.S.: the memoirs of Ulysses S. Grant.

It Fits You to a "T"

A brief history of the most popular shirt in the world.

You Be the Judge

T-shirts have been around so long that nobody knows for sure where they originated or how they got their name. One theory: They were first worn by longshoremen who loaded tea from the merchant ships in

Annapolis, Maryland, during the 17th century. They became known as "tea shirts" and eventually "T-shirts."

Another theory: They were invented by the British Royal Family for use by sailors in the Royal Navy. According to that version "the monarchy ordered sailors to sew sleeves on their undershirts to spare royalty the unseemly experience of witnessing an armada of armpits. Ergo, the shirt shaped like the letter T."

Undershirts Are Sunk

T-shirts were part of American life as early as 1913, when the U.S. Navy added crew-necked cotton under-shirts to its uniform. But they were generally limited to military use. To most American men, the only *real* undershirt was the sleeveless variety, "with over-the-shoulder straps, a deep neck and totally exposed armpits."

These however, were dealt a seri-ous blow in 1934 by actor Clark

Gable. In the Oscar-winning film *It Happened One Night*, Gable took off his shirt . . . and wasn't wearing anything underneath.

"Hardly a young man from coast to coast would be caught wearing one after that," Jim Murray writes in the *Los Angeles Times*. "It almost wrecked an industry, put people out of work."

By then, the T-shirt's transition from underwear to outerwear was already under way, and in the early 1930s, some sports shops began selling shirts with university insignias on them. But they were still primarily considered undershirts. In 1938 Sears, Roebuck & Co. added the "gob-style" short-sleeved undershirts (U.S. sailors were known as "gobs") to its catalog. Price: 24 cents apiece. They sold poorly—it was still too soon after the Gable fiasco.

T-shirt Fashion

It wasn't until World War II that
T-shirts really began to take hold in
American culture. Each branch of the
military issued millions of "skivvies"
in its own color, and in the Pacific
islands it was so hot that they were
virtually the only shirts that most
soldiers wore. When the fighting boys
returned home from the war, they
brought their taste for T-shirts with them.

"For a while," says J. D. Reed in *Smithsonian* magazine, "the T-shirt suggested the kind of crew-cut cleanliness and neatness indigenous to the new, postwar suburbs." Then in 1951, the movies struck again: Marlon Brando electrified audiences by wearing a skin-tight T-shirt in Tennessee Williams's *A Street Car Named Desire*. The actor's rippling muscles "gave the garment a sexual je ne sais quoi from which America has never recovered," writes one critic.

"Elvis Presley cheered it on, sneering in a T-shirt and leather jacket. And James Dean perpetuated the Attitude-with-a-T look in *Rebel Without a Cause* in 1955."

By the end of the 1950s, the T-shirt was no longer just a piece of underwear—it was a fashion statement. Today the American T-shirt industry sells over a billion T-shirts a year. The average American owns 25 of them.

Strange Celebrity Lawsuits

The Plaintiff: Mark Twain
The Defendant: Estes and Lauriat Publishing Co.
The Lawsuit: In 1876 the Canadian publishers pirated the text of Twain's book *Tom Sawyer* and put out a low-priced edition. It cut into legitimate U.S. sales and deprived Twain of royalties. When he wrote *The Adventures of Huckleberry Finn* in 1884, he was

determined to prevent a recurrence. He decided to publish *Huckleberry Finn* himself . . . but hold off printing it until he had orders for 40,000 copies. That way, the book pirates wouldn't have a chance to undercut him.

Yet somehow, Estes and Lauriat got hold of a manuscript and started selling a pirated edition two months *before* Twain's authorized edition was available. Livid, Twain sued them. **The Verdict:** Believe it or not, Twain lost the case. He issued this state-

Marriage Proposal

Who Said It: John Alden
Speaking For: Myles Standish
What Happened: As military leader of the pilgrims, Capt. Myles Standish was fearless. With ladies, however, he was the opposite. Standish was so afraid of expressing his love to Priscilla Mullens that he asked his young friend Alden to do it for him. The only problem: Alden was also in love with Mullens. Nonetheless, he

went off to proclaim Standish's love to the woman, keeping his own a secret.

As it happened, Mullens harbored her own secret feelings for Alden. When Alden delivered Standish's proposal instead, legend has it she replied, "Why don't you speak for yourself, John?"

Note: Mullens married Alden. Standish supposedly went into the woods for a few days and sulked. He eventually got over it.

Historic Speech

Who Said It: Norman Shelley
Speaking For: Winston Churchill
What Happened: A week after the demoralizing defeat of British and French troops by Germany at Dunkirk in 1940, Prime Minister Winston Churchill made one of the most stirring radio addresses in history. Speaking to the English public, he declared, in no uncertain terms, that the British would not fold.

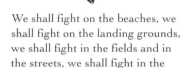

We shall fight on the beaches, we shall fight on the landing grounds, we shall fight in the fields and in the streets, we shall fight in the hills; we shall never surrender.

Historians say that this specific speech provided the morale boost that helped England summon the strength to continue the war effort . . . and ultimately win.

But Churchill didn't make the speech. He was "too busy to appear on the radio," so he asked Shelley to fill in — an actor who had perfected the Churchillian delivery to such a degree that few people could pick out which voice was Shelley's and which was Churchill's.

Let's Play Ballbuster!

Ballbuster
Product: No joke—the Mego Toy Co. introduced it in 1976 as "a family game that's loads of fun." It consisted of wire stalks attached to a gridlike base. Each was topped with a hinged red plastic ball. The object, according to Mego, was to "use your balls to bust your opponent's, if you can. Break 'em all and you're a winner!"
Problem: Somehow, Mego thought it

could get away with the name. But the first preview of the Ballbuster TV commercial—shown to buyers from major toy and department stores—ended that illusion. The ad showed a family playing the game, after which the husband turned to his wife and said, "Honey, you're a *real* ball buster!" "The stunned silence that followed triggered the first suspicions that Ballbuster was not destined to displace Parcheesi in the pantheon of classic games."

A Brief History of Bugs Bunny

Who's your favorite cartoon character? Ear's ours.

Impressive Stats

Bugs Bunny is the world's most popular rabbit:

- Since 1939, he has starred in more than 175 films.

• He's been nominated for three Oscars, and won one—in 1958, for "Knighty Knight, Bugs" (with Yosemite Sam).

• Every year from 1945 to 1961, he was voted "top animated character" by movie theater owners (when they still showed cartoons in theaters).

• In 1985 he became only the second cartoon character to be given a star on the Hollywood Walk of

Fame (Mickey Mouse was the first).

• For almost 30 years, starting in 1960, he had one of the top-rated shows on Saturday-morning TV.

• In 1976, when researchers polled Americans on their favorite characters, real and imaginary, Bugs came in second . . . behind Abraham Lincoln.

Looney Trivia

• The name "Looney Tunes" is a takeoff on Walt Disney's popular 1930s cartoon series, "Silly Symphonies."

• The real name of the Looney Tunes theme song is "The Merry-Go-Round Broke Down." It's a pop tune from the 1930s.

• The first Looney Tune, "Sinking

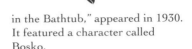

in the Bathtub," appeared in 1930.
It featured a character called
Bosko.

Random Facts

Cost, in parts and labor, for an
Academy Award Oscar statuette:
about $300.

Odds of being injured by a toilet seat
in your lifetime: 1 in 6,500.

What do rabbits and horses have in common? They can't vomit.

What's a *melcryptovestimentaphiliac*? Someone who compulsively steals ladies underwear.

One mother shark can give birth to as many as 70 baby sharks per litter.

In Venice, Venetian blinds are known as "Persian blinds."

What do gorillas and house cats have in common? Both purr.

Benjamin Franklin gave guitar lessons.

A hibernating bear can go as long as six months without a bathroom break.

again, so had the Erie Canal, and that wonder of the world was nearly finished, wasn't it? Besides, if it wasn't true, why would he publicly declare that the mayor had authorized him to handle the project?

What Happened: Lozier began signing up hundreds of laborers for the task, offering triple wages to anyone willing to saw underwater. He directed blacksmiths and carpenters to begin designing the 100-foot saws and 250-foot oars needed to saw the island and row it out to sea. He also arranged for the construction of barracks and a mess hall for his laborers, and the delivery of 500 cattle, 500 hogs, and 3,000 chickens, so his workers would have plenty to eat.

After two months of planning, the date arrived for construction to begin. Scores of laborers, carpenters, blacksmiths, butchers, and animals—as well as a marching band and hundreds of onlookers—arrived at Spring Street and Bowery to see the historic project get under way. About the only people who didn't show up were Lozier and his accomplices, who'd suddenly left town "on account of their health."

They were actually holed up in Brooklyn, and although there was talk of having them arrested, Alexander Klein writes in *Grand Deception*, "no one seemed willing to make a complaint to the authorities or admit that he had been duped, and Lozier went scot-free."

The Riddler

What's white and black and read in the middle? These pages of riddles. The answers follow.

1. What unusual natural phenomenon is capable of speaking in any language?

2. A barrel of water weighs 20 pounds. What do you have to add to make it weigh 12 pounds?

3. Before Mount Everest was discovered, what was the highest mountain on earth?

4. What word starts with an "e," ends with an "e," and usually contains one letter?

5. Forward I am heavy, but backward I am not. What am I?

6. He has married many women, but has never been married. Who is he?

7. How many bricks does it take to complete a building made of brick?

8. How many of each animal did Moses take on the ark?

9. How many times can you subtract the number 5 from 25?

10. If you have it, you want to share it. If you share it, you don't have it. What is it?

11. In Okmulgee, Oklahoma, you cannot take a picture of a man with a wooden leg. Why not?

12. The more you have of it, the less you see. What is it?

13. The more you take, the more you leave behind. What are they?

14. The one who makes it, sells it. The one who buys it, never uses it. The one who uses it, never knows

that he's using it. What is it?

15. What can go up a chimney down but can't go down a chimney up?

16. What crime is punishable if attempted, but is not punishable if committed?

17. What happened in the middle of the 20th century that will not happen again for 4,000 years?

18. What is the center of gravity?

19. What question can you never honestly answer "yes" to?

20. You can't keep this until you have given it.

Answers — The Riddler

1. An echo.
2. Holes.
3. Mount Everest.

4. Envelope.

5. A ton.

6. A priest.

7. Only one . . . the last one.

8. Zero . . . Noah took animals on the ark, not Moses.

9. Only once. After the first calculation, you will be subtracting 5 from 20, then 5 from 15, and so on.

10. A secret.

11. You can't take a picture with a wooden leg . . . . You need a camera!

12. Darkness.

13. Footsteps.
14. A coffin.
15. An umbrella.
16. Suicide.
17. The year 1961. It reads the same upside down. Won't happen again until the year 6009.
18. The letter "V."
19. "Are you asleep?"
20. A promise.

The Dustbin of History

Think your heroes will go down in history for something they've done? Don't count on it. These folks were VIPs in their time . . . but they're forgotten now. They've been swept into the Dustbin of History.

Forgotten Figure: John "Bet-a-Million" Gates, a compulsive gambler in the late 1800s, who once tried to bet $1 million on a horse at Saratoga

Race Course, "causing bookmakers to run for cover"

Claim to Fame: Gates started out as a $30-a-month barbed-wire salesman, but after a few years of skilled gambling, built a $50 million fortune. He was notorious for parting robber barons from their money, taking millions from Andrew Carnegie and relieving financier J. P. Morgan of $15 million on a single bet. Beating capitalists at their own game—making money—made him a hero with the public.

Gates's luck eventually ran out and he lost everything in a bet with J. P. Morgan . . . or almost everything. Gates reportedly got down on his knees and begged Morgan not to bankrupt him; Morgan relented — on the condition that Gates leave New York forever.

Gates had to accept. He moved to Texas and invested what little money he had left in drilling for oil. Most of the wells he dug were dry holes, but formance money and were working at a supermarket in Charlotte, North Carolina. They died within hours of each other from influenza in 1960.

Random Facts

The fishing reel was invented around the year A.D. 300.

Estimated value of a single pair of Elvis's underpants: $1,300.

In 1797 James Hetherington invented the top hat and wore it in public. He was arrested for disturbing the peace.

Food for thought: Peanut butter sandwiches weren't popular until the 1920s.

It takes 720 peanuts to make a pound of peanut butter.

How do you know when a turkey is panicking? That's the only time it whistles.

What do whales and buffalo have in common? Both stampede.

At last count, Minnesota had 99 lakes named Mud Lake.

On average, adults have 2 gallons of air in the space between their skin and their clothes.

The ancient Greeks played cards. In those days, aces were known as "dogs."

Odd Jobs

Looking for an exciting new job? Here's a list of the most unusual-sounding occupations we could find.

Killer Bee Hunter. Your mission: Track down Africanized "killer" bees, which are migrating north from

Central America, and destroy them before they can take up residence in North America.

Chicken Shooter. Fire dead chickens out of a cannon at aircraft to see what kind of damage occurs.

Mother Repairer. It's not what you think. It actually entails repairing metal phonograph record "mothers" (the master from which records are pressed) by removing dirt and nickel particles from the grooves.

Anthem Man. A unique profession: King Alfonso of Spain was tone deaf . . . he employed one man whose job was to alert him when the Spanish national anthem was playing (so he would know when to salute).

Worm Collector. Get ready to crawl through grass at night with a flashlight, to catch the best worms for fishing. Tip: Grab them in the middle to avoid bruising them.

Weed Farmer. If you like gardening, here's a change of pace: *grow* weeds . . . then sell them to chemical companies for herbicide research.

Pig Manure Sniffer. Workers try to recognize chemical markers in manure so researchers can determine which foods make pig manure so foul-smelling. Women only, because estrogen increases sensitivity to smell.

Sewage Diver. Put on a diving suit and plunge into a sewage-containment vat.

Animal Chauffeur. We've heard of only one—a guy named Stephen May. His "limousine" is equipped with, among other things: a blanketed floor, eight-inch color television, stereo speakers, and silk flowers.

Flush Tester. A gold star from Uncle John to the gallant professionals who test toilet-bowl standards by trying to flush rags down various toilets.

Armpit Sniffer. Enough said.

The Joke's On Us

Americans tend to overlook an important side to our love affair with celebrities—they're always trying to sell us something: an idea, image, or product. And many of them don't mind lying to us, either. Here are a few examples.

For Sale: A Cherished Possession

In the early 1900s, Bat Masterson, legendary Wild West lawman, became a New York sportswriter. Because he needed the money, he reluctantly agreed to sell his famous shotgun—the "gun that tamed the West."

The Truth: He actually bought old guns at pawnshops or junk stores, carved notches in them (one for each "kill"), and sold them to admirers for a tidy profit. Each time, he swore it was the authentic gun he'd used in Dodge City.

**For Sale:
An Intellectual Image**

In 1961 an article in *Time* magazine
helped convince Americans that
they'd elected an exceptionally bright
man as president. It reported that
JFK had taken a course in something
called "speed-reading" and could zip
through an amazing 1,200 words per
minute. It became common knowledge—and part of his mystique—that
he could read through a whole book
in one sitting.
The Truth: The number was concocted
by Kennedy and *Time* reporter Hugh

Sidey. First, JFK told Sidey he could read 1,000 words a minute. Upon reflection, however, he decided that number sounded too low. "How about 1,200?" Sidey asked. "Okay," Kennedy replied. And that's what was printed. Actually, JFK never finished the speed-reading course he took and, at best, could read 800 wpm (still a lot, but not as impressive).

For Sale:
A Folksy White House Tradition

It was a Yuletide tradition during the Reagan presidency. Gathering with reporters, the Great Communicator would ceremoniously light the National Christmas Tree on the Mall in Washington, D.C., by pushing a button from inside the White House. **The Truth:** The button wasn't connected to anything—a Park Service employee actually lit the tree. The press found out by accident in 1989, when President Bush went to the tree site and lit it in person. Bush's press have offered $100,000 for the remains of Michael Jackson's nose.")

• was so obsessed with his chimp, Bubbles, that he was learning "monkey language" to communicate with him.

Even more than his music, the constant stream of reports on Jackson's weirdnesses made him a pervasive presence in pop culture. Everyone talked about him.

The Truth: The stories were all

false—concocted, it turns out, by Jackson himself. According to one report, Jackson had "learned early how little truth means when seeking publicity" back when he was in the Jackson 5. In private, he even "began reading biographies of hokum-master P. T. Barnum for ideas."

Trick Shots: Famous Faked Photos

If there's a lesson to be learned from

these historic phonies, it's that people believe what they want to believe. In the face of overwhelming logic — or even solid contrary evidence — people have clung to the notion that the real truth was revealed in these photographs.

Fairy Tale

Famous Photo: English fairies
Trick Shot: In 1917 Sir Arthur Conan Doyle, "an ardent believer in

the occult," announced that, just as he'd always believed, sprites, gnomes, and other types of fairies really did exist. His proof: photographs of fairies taken by 16-year-old Elsie Wright and her 10-year-old cousin Frances Griffiths. "The pictures showed the girls by a wooded stream, with winged sprites and gnomes who danced and pranced and tooted on pipes," Michael Farquhar writes in the *Washington Post*. "Several of the photography experts who examined the pictures declared them free of superimposition or retouching," and the photos, backed by Conan Doyle's testament to their authenticity launched a national fairy craze.

The Real Picture: "In 1983, the girls, by then old women, admitted that they had posed with paper cutouts supported by hatpins."

Un-Loch-ing the Truth

Famous Photo: Loch Ness monster
Trick Shot: On April 19, 1934, Robert Wilson and a companion were walking along the shore of Loch Ness when the friend suddenly shouted, "My God, it's the monster!" Wilson grabbed his camera and snapped a quick photograph of what appears to be "a sea beast with a humpback and a long neck"—the legendary Loch Ness monster, an elusive creature

Note: Hard-core believers are unimpressed by the revelation. "Eyewitness accounts still suggest that there is something powerful in the loch," says Adrian Shine, founder of a group called The Loch Ness Project.

Uncle John's Page of Lists

For years, the BRI has had a file full of lists. We've never been sure what to do with them . . . until now.

3 Celebrities Who Say They've Seen a UFO

1. Muhammad Ali
2. Jimmy Carter
3. William Shatner

7 Weird Place Names

1. Peculiar, Missouri
2. Smut Eye, Alabama
3. Loudville, Massachusetts
4. Disco, Illinois
5. Yeehaw Junction, Florida
6. Slaughter Beach, Delaware
7. Humptulips, Washington

3 Men Known by Their Middle Names

1. James Paul McCartney
2. William Clark Gable
3. Ruiz Fidel Castro

4 Words Nobody Uses Anymore

1. Podge ("To walk slowly and heavily")
2. Roinous ("Mean and nasty")
3. Battologist ("Someone who point-

lessly repeats themselves")
4. Battologist ("Someone who point-lessly repeats themselves")

3 Most Prized Autographs

1. Shakespeare (6 are known to exist)
2. Christopher Columbus (8 exist)
3. Julius Caesar (None are known to exist)

Random Facts

President Grover Cleveland's nickname was "Uncle Jumbo."

If you visit, bring sunblock. Neptune's summer is 40 years long.

Sloths even sneeze slowly. And they give birth upside down. Slowly.

Why do we say something is out of whack? What is a whack?

If a pig loses its voice, is it disgruntled?

Why are a wise man and a wise guy opposites?

Why does the word "lisp" have a "s" in it?

If Fred Flintstone knew that the large

order of ribs would tip his car over, why did he order them at the end of every show?

If Superman is so smart, why does he wear underpants over his trousers?

Animal Myths

Here are a few examples of things that some people believe about animals . . . but just aren't true.

Myth: Bats are blind.
Fact: Bats aren't blind. But they have evolved as nocturnal hunters, and can see better in half-light than in day-light.

Myth: Monkeys remove fleas in each other's fur during grooming.
Fact: Monkeys don't have fleas. They're removing dead skin—which they eat.

Myth: Male seahorses can become

pregnant and give birth.

Fact: What actually happens is this: The female seahorse expels eggs into the male's brood pouch, where they are fertilized. And while the male does carry the gestating embryos until they are born 10 days later, he doesn't feed them through a placenta or similar organ (as had previously been thought). Instead, the embryos feed off of the nourishment in the egg itself—food provided by the female. Basically, the male acts as an incubator.

Myth: Porcupines can shoot their quills when provoked.

Fact: A frightened porcupine tends to run from danger. If a hunter catches it, though, a porcupine will tighten its skin to make the quills stand up . . . ready to lodge in anything that touches them.

Myth: Whales spout water.

Fact: Whales actually exhale *air* through their blowholes. This creates a mist or fog that looks like a water spout.

Myth: Moths eat clothes.
Fact: Not exactly. Moths lay their eggs on your clothes, which eventually develop into larvae. It's the larvae that eat tiny parts of your clothes; adult moths do not eat cloth.

Myth: Bumblebee flight violates the laws of aerodynamics.
Fact: Nothing that flies violates the laws of aerodynamics.

Classic Trivia

Alexander Dumas, author of *The Three Musketeers* and *The Count of Monte Cristo*, always wrote his novels on blue paper, his poetry on yellow paper, and his nonfiction on rose-colored paper. Always—to do otherwise, he explained, was "unspeakable."

Strange Animal Lawsuits

In the Middle Ages, it was not unusual for animals to be put on trial as if they could understand human laws. These lawsuits were serious affairs.

The Plaintiffs: Vineyard growers in St.-Julien, France
The Defendants: Weevils
The Lawsuit: In 1545 angry growers testified to a judge that the weevils

were eating and destroying their crops. According to one source: "Legal indictments were drawn, and the insects actually defended in court."

The Verdict: Since the weevils were obviously eating the crops, they were found guilty. In 1546 a proclamation was issued by the judge demanding that the weevils desist . . . and amazingly, they did. The farmers weren't bothered by the weevils again until

1587. Once more, the insects were put on trial; however, the outcome is unknown.

The Plaintiffs: The people of Mayenne, France

The Defendant: Mosquitoes

The Lawsuit: In the 1200s, a swarm of mosquitoes were indicted as a public nuisance by the people of the town. When the bugs failed to answer the summons, the court appointed a lawyer to act on their behalf.

The Verdict: The lawyer did such a good job pleading their case that the court took pity. The judge banished them, but gave them a patch of real estate outside town where they would be allowed to swarm in peace "forever."

The Plaintiff: The city of Basel, Switzerland

The Defendant: A rooster

The Lawsuit: In 1474 the rooster was accused of being (or helping) a sorcerer. The reason, according to the prosecutor: it had laid eggs . . . and as everyone knows, an egg laid by a rooster is prized by sorcerers. On top of that, it was shown that "Satan employed witches to hatch such eggs, from which proceeded winged serpents most dangerous to mankind."

The rooster's lawyer admitted it had laid an egg, but contended that "no injury to man or beast had resulted." And besides, laying an egg is an involuntary act, he said, so the law shouldn't punish it.

Since, by law, the rats were entitled to protection to and from court, the plaintiffs "should be required to post a bond" that would be forfeited if the cats attacked the rats on their way to court.

The Verdict: Unknown, but the publicity from the case helped Chassenée to establish a reputation as a sharp lawyer. In fact, many historians now regard him as one of France's greatest lawyers.

The Plaintiff: The Grand Vicar of Valence, France

The Defendants: Caterpillars inhabiting his diocese

The Lawsuit: In 1584 the Grand Vicar excommunicated the insects for causing destruction to crops, and ordered them to appear before him. When they didn't appear, a lawyer was appointed to defend them.

The Verdict: The lawyer argued his case, but lost. The caterpillars were banished from the diocese. "When the caterpillars failed to leave, the trial continued until the short-lived caterpillars died off. The Vicar was then credited with having miraculously exterminated them."

Keep on Truckin'

According to a poll by American Tours International the "most unexpected" (and unintentional) tourist attractions in the U.S. for foreign visitors are truck stops. Foreigners view truck drivers as "the last cowboys" and like to visit their eating places. Another big attraction: I-90 in South Dakota, "a blacktop with few towns for hundreds of miles."

BRI's Flatulence Hall of Fame

It used to be that no one talked about farts . . . now, it's no big deal. You can't get away from it. Which is fine by us. Here is the very first section honoring people and institutions that have made an art out of passing gas. (By the way—if this is your favorite part of the book, we recommend a tome called *Who Cut the Cheese?* by Jim Dawson.)

Honoree: Caryn Johnson, a.k.a. Whoopi Goldberg
Notable Achievement: First Hollywood star named after frequent farting

True Story: In her autobiography, Goldberg says she came up with the stage name Whoopi because she "frequently passed gas and sounded like a walking whoopee cushion."

Honoree: Taoism
Notable Achievement: Most interesting philosophy about farts
True Story: A 1996 BBC-TV program about the first Chinese emperor, reported that "Chinese Taoists believe everyone is allotted a certain amount

of air at birth which is important to conserve. Belching and farting are considered to shorten one's life. Taoists therefore carefully control their diet, avoiding food which leads to flatulence."

Honoree: King Ahmose of Egypt
Notable Achievement: Most effective use of a fart as a political statement
True Story: In 568 B.C., King Apries of Egypt sent a trusted general named Amasis to put down a mutiny among

his troops. But when Amasis got there, the troops offered to make him their leader instead . . . and he accepted.

King Apries couldn't believe it. He sent a respected advisor named Patarbemis to bring Amasis back. Amasis responded to the king's entreaties by raising himself from his saddle and farting. Then he told Patarbemis to "carry that back to Apries." Unfortunately, the king was so enraged by the message that he had Patarbemis's nose and ears hacked off. Committing such a barbarous act against such a respectable man was the last straw for many Egyptians—they turned pro-Amasis. With their support, Amasis's troops attacked and defeated Aprises's army. **Note:** Amasis became King Ahmose and reigned for 44 years from 569 to 525 B.C., which modern historians call one of Egypt's most prosperous periods.

Honoree: Richard Magpiong, a career criminal

Notable Achievement: The ultimate self-incriminating fart

True Story: In 1995 the residents of a home on Fire Island (near New York City) were awakened by a noise. They got up and looked around, but couldn't find anyone. They were about to go back to bed when, according to the *New York Daily News*, "they heard the sound of a muffled fart." Magpiong was discovered hiding in a closet and was held until the police arrived.

Honoree: Edward De Vere, the seventh earl of Oxford and a courtier in Queen Elizabeth's court

Notable Achievement: Craziest overreaction to a fart

True Story: De Vere accidentally farted while bowing to the queen. He was so embarrassed that he left England and did not return for seven years. When he got back, the queen pooh-poohed the whole affair. "My Lord," she reportedly said, welcoming him back, "I had forgot the Fart."

Honoree: Spike Jones and His City Slickers

Notable Achievement: Best-selling fart record

True Story: According to *Who Cut the Cheese?*: "During World War II, Bluebird Records released a disc called 'Der Fuehrer's Face' by Spike Jones and His City Slickers (an orchestra noted for their parodying pop tunes), only a few months after the U.S. joined the war. Jones's band, armed with rubber razzers to create flabby farting noises, [created] a zany gas attack on Adolf Hitler: 'And we'll Heil! [*fart!*] Heil [*fart!*] right in der Fuehrer's face!'" It sold a million and a half copies in the U.S. and Great Britain.

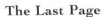

The Last Page

Well, we're out of space, and when you've gotta go, you've gotta go. Meanwhile, remember:

Go with the flow.